AF263727

From North Of The 49th

Poems of Social and Historical Narratives, And

Some Personal Reflections of a Canadian

Jack Nanaimo

Contents

Dedication

To my wife and family.

To my friend Brian M. of 50 plus years, a lover of poetry, who told me one of the responsibilities of poets is to write truths about the signs of our times. I hope in some small measure I have been able to do so.

Acknowledgments

To the many people I have sent these poems to over the past three years who have provided many constructive comments and encouragement having borne up with my "poem of the day" emails.

About the Author

Retired after a career in business, my wife and I bought a farm where we grew organic crops for a number of years. The poems reflect personal memories, and observations on nature, events of our time, and history. There is no poetic format or established poetic structure followed. The writings reflect only the thoughts that occurred to me at the time the poem was written.

North Of The 49th

There in the north reaching the eternal sun
Lying between oceans Canada's lands have spun
Mountains and plains and forests, her beauty stuns
An anchor for the world her sanctity unsung

She has it within her, with resources intact
A breadbasket for the world, she need never look back
No bombs or invaders have ever attacked
Her detractors lie within, giving her aimless whacks

Do not all of us see where we stand in the world
When internal strife from little voices leaves us uncurled
And the vision of Canada is left foundered and swirled
When idle views of some aren't curbed and furled

Where else on the planet do people have it so good
Yet some want to split, leaving us provincial driftwood
Shrill voices of a few not thinking how she stood
Its time her greatness came out of the woods

Deadly pipsqueaks around the world who can't live but for wars
Leave your world's terrors far from our shores
United people in our nation will give vision to our corps
For if the world falls asunder Canadians still will soar

Chapter 1
British Columbia

Nanaimo

West to Nanaimo where I was born
Long ago in the midst of war
A city so beautiful as any could have sworn
There looking seaward as we walked her shore

Up on Kennedy Street overlooking the Sea
Way down the hill to the wharves in the bay
The ferry to Vancouver was waiting in place
And boats and tugs and logs floated gay

What a home for a kid in times past away
Mountains and seas and forests from Eon's hands
Clear skies and shipyards and Departure Bay
Swimming in tides and walking on sea sands

Is it still the same seventy years moving past
Are those of Vancouver Island as happy in the land
As we once were in the last century so vast
Ah, memories so big when the mind does command

Williams Lake Stampede

Williams Lake B.C.

What a place was Williams Lake
North from Vancouver, where the Cariboo spans
A great stampede there every year to make
For rodeo times in cow country land

We camped there one year
For the rodeo and horse races
A Hundred teepees on the hill appeared
Smoke from their fires wafting our places

Thousands of visitors to watch the great skills
Races and riding and kids competing like mad
With hair flying back from the speed and the thrills
I watched over the stalls for the bulls to go bad

A whole side of beef was roasted in fire
Covered in dirt for a day over a hot coal bed
A sandwich made crisp with blackened beef to inspire
In a half loaf of bread for a buck a head

The town had a boardwalk to keep out the flood
Of mud in the fifties when life's colour was on show
Memories remembered of youth that was tugged
By Cariboo Country from a lifetime ago

Now when I order a steak when going out for dinner
They ask Pittsburg, or Chicago, well done, or rare
I reply this is Canada, we know how to deliver
Make it Williams Lake charred for great steak fare.

4

The Canadian Rockies

I remember the Rockies when I was a kid
which surrounded BC in massive grids

Upwards upwards every foot a new sight
On to the peaks lost among clouds of white

Rocky and tumbled with hard black granite
Trees on slopes growing in dark green palettes

One could stand on the Great Divide impressed
Splitting the mountain roof to the east and west

Waters in the east heading north to the Arctic
With western flows plunging down to the Pacific

Valleys between ranges holding fruits and gardens
And dry vistas heading north with the grasses and sages

Long lakes in the centre sparkling like fountains
Farms on their shores rising up the steep mountains

Glaciers retreating in the northern valleys
Cold waters flowing down in rushing alleys

Ghost towns and mines long since abandoned
Harbouring burnouts left from riches demanded

Giant trees and lakes and oceans surrounding
Farming and fishing and lumbering and mining

Giant mountains in BC's tranquility abounding
Protected by oceans, the surf ever-pounding

Ferries and ships and trade ever-expanding
British Columbia is there in western Canada anchoring

Gabriola

An Island off Nanaimo in the Salish Sea
Reached by an old ferry packed with cars like sardines
Gabriola was home when we docked at her quay
A beautiful island covered with magnificent fir trees

My grandmother lived there for many years
In a little house she built herself by the firs
Sawing and hammering and placing the beams
Alone on an island through my early teens

A little house with her art hung to be seen
A mural of dancers gamboling naked on the green
A little woman with a brush painting scene after scene
An artist born in Truro and a grandmother never mean

A few feet to the west was an abandoned brick yard
With little steel tracks running through some old kilns
We rode the rails for there weren't any guards
The old switches worked and the carts moved us like kings

Learning to swim in an inlet on the west
Taylor Bay is still there with its beautiful sand
A view from space shows how the Bay was blessed
Giving swimmers and children quiet peace on the strand

Isolated and separate from Vancouver Island
A place where some moved to be quiet and alone
Away from the bustle for a new life in a garland
Calmness and quiet healing minds like a bloodstone

British Columbia Flumes

The British Columbia Flumes were mighty rivers of wood
Man-made movers carrying cut forests to the sea
With fast-moving water a log was carried through
From a giant felled using two-man crosscut crews

Those saws were so sharp and precision-tuned
Just like a laser but made with file, set, and hammer
Sharp tools helped lumberjacks whenever they were used
To saw through a tree big in ancient diameter

The saw was a crown with its jewel the axe
Treated like royalty to ease the work of muscles
Bound up when put away and treasured when relaxed
Handled with reverence shining like gossamer bubbles.

At height the water source was tuned and harnessed
The downward flow channeled in a man-made torrent
To curve in long flumes down mountainsides
Moving logs to salt water after the forest's death warrant

No more do the flumes of the Big Timber heft
As the ancient forests remembered mostly ran out
Now trucks, mere burros, are all that is left
Moving Douglas fir, Red cedar, and Sitka spruce about

It should be remembered when mountains were raw
Every flume had a forest on a mountainside that awed
And every forest was cut and is now gone by the saw
In the "hard march of man" who seldom withdraws (1)

What an experience for millennia to have heard the giants whisper
For those living in the green mantle who were spirit-blessed
Crafting split timber in planks from cedars and fir
And totems of spirits gazing seaward in the Pacific Northwest

No more can we see through a forest so ancient
The shelters and structures and canoes and tools
Unless through the stumps that man created
Or until another thousand years pass leaving the trees unbruised

(1) The hard march of man is a quote that stuck with me when,
long years ago, I read Churchill's memoirs of the Second World
War.

Lumber Carriers of Victoria

On many Victoria streets
Lumber carriers hauled many board feet
Crossing tracks and roads they carted
From yard to yard they rolled and darted

Carrying milled lumber moving fast and nimbly
Between cars and bikes and people so quickly

Millions of board feet of lumber that gleamed
Beauty wood for houses and bridges and ships
Free of knots was number one for cedar and fir
Sawdust from cuts blown in basements to heat homes

The big trees yielded all
From once great timber halls
Cut down and milled by billions of falls
Big Timber was a diamond from the ancient forest halls

Chapter 2
Water Forests Oceans Land Sky

The Daffodil

Blooming here in the east in the March upswing
Between gusts of snow and freezing rain
Are daffodil blooms reflecting a sunny new spring
Yellow with their light inside by a window pane

Long ago in February, on warm Vancouver Island
Yellow blooms grew like rising melodies on a piano
Bursting with colour as the first of the diamonds
So you know it's spring in Victoria and Nanaimo

Cheery blossoms blooming in season's routine
Earthy bulbs every year become garden queens
Free in warm earth to bring us spirits serene
Lightening the mind with yellow and green

Green With New Blood

Life in the forests green with new blood
Climbing for light in a vertical flood
Water and rain helping the new buds
Wind in the trees where leaves are drummed

Rivers plunge down from the rocky plateau
Glimpsed through the forest where sparkles shimmer
In spring, torrents of water and spray are aglow
Or slow over pools where quiet murmurs ripple

The colours of fall cause the blue of the river
To glow in the sun as the view gets much clearer
The reds of the maples dying out to yellow silver
Tree trunks and branches seen in the river's mirror

In winter with no leaves to obscure the sight
All can be seen as time gets closer to freezing
Ice will be formed so no water flows in the night
Eyes seeing white as winter snows are streaming

Waiting for spring again to see bursting buds
The trees filling out shadowing the river's sight
As life in the trees turns green with new blood
Back waiting for the colours of fall's frostbite

Ensure our forests are growing in a flood
Without them the world will have less oxygen to derive
So whenever a tree turns green with new blood
Its a sign our forests are thriving, and man will survive

Cathedral Grove, British Columbia

What did he in the dugout see
Paddling the coast with the Spirit's hymn
From ice and snow in the north
South to Green life on the Pacific rim

For eons and eons in towering transcendence
The cedar and fir giants rose to light
Young when Caesar and Charlemagne ascended
But standing now in perilous might

Rooted still, in a grove of divinity
Mighty and strong through centuries
Protected by nature but now no serenity
At risk because of man's destructive infamy

He watched for long days, riding the waves
Seeing life on the coast through the evergreens
Which harboured the heirs of the past
Giving host to the coming of new dreams

Now only a remnant of magnificence left
The giant trees safe in Cathedral Grove
For memories not lost but blessed
With the warmth of the Giant's souls

One September Morning

There was a frost last night glowing in the city lights
As the temperature dropped and fog froze in whites
On branches and puddles, crisping rain into ice
A frozen carpet seen looking over a fire's flames at night
But the gloom of the evening was made fresh and so bright
As art forms in bright ice covered the trees till' daylight

As the sun rose in the east in a climbing symphony
Sunbeams through icicles were reflecting rainbows
As ever the sun rose into full-day splendour
The carpet of crystals could be seen onwards forever
Calming the eye as it looked at the beauty in the light
Whoever thought ice could warm the spirit in delight

Splinters of Light

Low in the east is the Pleiades Constellation
Brilliant splinters of light when seen by the rotation
Of the Earth when they rise in heaven's narration
Causing minds to roam through black vistas in ovation

Do thoughts ever rise without stars as light
Or are they subdued to shut out the dark at night
But when man gathered wood and set it alight
Then thoughts became sparks rising like stars in sight

Seen through some binoculars in towering heights
Is a carpet of stars from the infinite in the universe's might
Brilliant, brilliant, to the mind of man at their sight
No wonder dreamers dream by those splinters of light

(From the author's collection)

Lighted Streets Of Snow

Driving through the city at night
On snowy streets in endless delight
Lights from houses and lamps excite
Warm in the car on a starry night

Road after road around every corner
New sights there in the black of night
Shadows appear from high street lights
And windows in houses shine out so bright

Where in the world where seasons don't differ
Can one see winter lighting the night
A season of Time when old senses are renewed
With the warmth of life in the night, so white

Canada Goose (in Haiku)

The Canada Goose

Flys high in long V patterns

Straight even at night

The Canadian V

Gracing our skies in V's out of sight
Flying high non-stop far into the night
On a course to the south in ancient foresight
Landing to rest at the end of the flight

Flying Canadians in our northern lands
Welcome in sight, flying in heavenly span
Wondrous they are in their high command
Of continents and skies and tundras in nature's plan

Should ever the Canada Goose cease to fly
Harbingers of seasons passing relentlessly by
Something will be lost without their wings in the sky
The equinoxes might not turn with man wondering why

Soon in the spring, the geese V's will head north
Their familiar calls echoing in the mountains of air
And nesting along waterways will allow life to come forth
To fly in endless formations as they rise high in their lair

The Cardinal

Waking to a symphonic song
A little bird's melody is drifting along
Perched on a pole or branch alone
His song fills the morning and all day long

Bright red and filled with music he calls the breeze
To deliver his song among all the trees
Through open windows you can hear his reprise
For all the world is his feathered diocese.

The Great Navigator

Along the roaring forties under the Southern Cross
Where winds blow free around the globe
A great navigator is flying the fringes of Antarctica
The albatross's home over the ocean's cold robe

Gone for months, gliding over the waves
Bad weather a detail in its flight as it braves
Its life over oceans far from shore and home
A model of free energy using wind power alone

Hovering low over the icy ocean caps
Cold spray never minded in its low-air attack
Hunting fish in the sea, never looking at maps
Gliding a foot high over waves in its ocean track

Circling the globe below the Southern Cross
Its circumnavigations of the world a testament to flight
Back to a lonely island only to give life
This long-lived wonder is a treasure in nature's light

Clouds

Where to begin when speaking of great clouds
How many in the past looked and sang
At the sky in the heavens to which they bowed
Did they get the words right about the glittering ranks

Marching, climbing in the eye, to the west
Shape-changing white gemstones rise in the sight
Tumbling, never to rest, new forms never stressed
As the dark surrounds they are there in the night

As the sky grows dark in the day to grey
Hard forms cover the sight as the sparks ignite
No shelter at sea as the wind screams 'Hey'
The winds are gods that the waves can't fight

Over the forests, oceans, prairies and mountains
The clouds race by forming towers that climb
To the horizon where the shadows ride
The clouds in the sunset to the sight sublime

Clouds stretch out over wide land vistas
Their towering peaks rise high not contained
The rain hits the slope and the fir trees strain
Through centuries, centuries, of clouds wind and rain

A spirit to the brain, the cloud water has traction
Rain of life for animals, forests and grain
Lakes, rivers, oceans and marine mansions
The food chain goes on never broken or strained

Tides

Tides, bubbling receding, but creeping ever closer
Up the sandy shore to little ocean pools

Filling them up with newfound saltwater
Salty and cool and clear as ice water

Minnows and crabs rush the watery perches
Hunting the new brought up by the tide

Turning on the moon as it fades in the sky
Tides back out again as it rotates away

Tidal reaches stretch out over wide shore vistas
Where beings of the earth gather and listen

Quiet sometimes with no screaming waters
Or hitting with force and moulding rock caverns

Calming and restful even in a storm
The play of tidewater is music in an art form

The Forest

South of the North Pole of cold-swept ice
Her lands reach up beyond the northern circle
Her nations white and green in frost-bitten nights
Stretching down to the Antarctic between oceans eternal

The mark of her trees is everywhere on the land
With majestic green swaths along rivers headed down
To oceans around her borders under Earth's command
Where Her trees reach up in continental green gowns

Where mountains appear under far-off skies
Where pastures and prairies grow food for the earth
Her name is The Forest, life's ally of allies
Whose growth is ancient and whose roots have given birth

The trees of her lands stand, embracing the future
Planted firmly in billions in her wide waiting spaces
We want no man's carnage, allowing negligent abuse
But need her, strong and growing, alive for the ages

The Ides of Spring

It's snowing today, driving hard into March
Getting closer to Spring's triumphal arch
Snow still here, although some rivers flow
And winds howl mightily as they forever blow

Daffodils have long begun to grow
Colouring the West Coast in golden rows
And buds are showing the green once stowed
Waiting patiently for the sun's spring light to glow

The corners are turning 'round and 'round
And plants are bursting to be let out of the ground
The seasons roll and never-ending life rebounds
And coming days will chime with spring's musical sound

Canadian Spring

Over the grey and white and dark earth belt
Sunbeams in the clouds make the earth so bright
For sunlit prisms of ice will soon heat and melt
And water will take on the reflection of light

The skies are clearing as light spreads so strong
Shadows following the sun from morning till night
As the sun warms the land beginning spring's song
Earth's colour is waiting to rise in day's light

As one walks among trees and hedges of stone
On carpets of grass becoming greener each day
The wildflowers wave happily in the earth now grown
Frozen prisms, once in ice now in flowering ballets

Bright sheets of flowers dancing where we reach
The whispering wind cradles petals all the hours
Beckoning onwards the journey that humbles any speech
In the might of the sun, the earth, and gentle rain showers

Earth, A Great Blue Jewel

The poem was inspired by the descriptions of Earth as a blue jewel by astronauts.

A gleam on an edge of the Milky Way
Orbiting in a system of gravitational might
Never-ending in the universe's billions of years
A chord in harmony in a starry symphony of nights
A great blue jewel in a sun's warmth, pulsing
With life, as it's oceans and clouds reflect light
Of a star in a galaxy giving eons of life

Chapter 3
Injustice

The Soldier Who Couldn't Fight Back

Ottawa, The National War Memorial, early winter 2022

The Tomb Of The Unknown Soldier
Was the sight of a desecration that smouldered

A Canadian who fought for the right to be free
Had no real choice but to bend his knee
When protesters insulted his sacred Tomb
For all the world to see

Humiliating Canada's Soldier who couldn't fight back

A First Nations Boy

A poem about Chanie Wenjack, who died trying to get away from a school in the Canadian Residential School System. While this poem is about Chanie, it can equally apply to all young children who bear the weight of injustice everywhere in the world.

I was only twelve but am now with my ancestors
I don't worry anymore about harsh cold nights

Our country so beautiful, full of water and trees
Wildlife abounded by rivers that surrounded
A land with colour as far as could be seen
Room for us all and no need to be grounded

Now I'm no longer around
My Dad was away north from the school in a pound
I wanted to go see him but was found on the ground
As I challenged the rule and froze and had to lay down

They finally broke that frightening chain bound 'round
Too late for me, though, since I'm now long dead
I'm living with my Dad here and at last, I'm unbound
Our vision is clear and we will no longer be bled

I don't think you judges had much of any vision
Your power roared when you had it and could use it
But not against all Canada's kids who didn't face your derision
Who were free at home and not state or religion-bitten

I too was a child of the Land but you didn't know it
I didn't either until found dead by the tracks
I didn't need you, nor did the tradition of ancients
None will forget your draconian acts

I wish I could have dreamed more without any fright
None who took me are covered with much glory
But as best I can, I hope all will be well tonight

Don't do it again, for you have no right
Molding others with unknown sight
Blind with righteous and religious might
An angry world might be watching and ignite

North from Inukjuak to the High Arctic

Families were recycled for fears of the Cold wars
Trading citizen's well-being to ease territorial fears
Officials weren't thinking of First Nation's sores
Doing whatever to them in those unjust years

What was the price to be paid for this tragedy
Moving the Inuit North to make a Cold War frontier
What frozen hearts of Canada permitted this brutality
Forcing families to the islands of Cornwallis and Ellesmere

One wonders sometimes why there is so much anger
Against those who called for that Inuit migration
In a tragedy enforced to create an Arctic anchor
Ordered by Ottawa mandarins far south in the nation

What lawmakers implemented this frightful extraction
For those in Ottawa was this but an abstraction
Going home at night to watch the hockey attraction
No time given to Inuit children in their Arctic action

The power elite didn't think in their mindless hysteric
Their actions bad, the intentions barbaric
The migration order was Imperial and without remorse
Shortsighted policy against First Nations and power enforced

Even our wildlife had rules for protection
But not those Inuit who Canada had forsaken
Who were deemed a symbol under law's subjugation

No more say those peoples who energized from those fears
In that Arctic disgrace dealt to Canada's Inuit peers

Poundmaker

Marked with a cairn the great chief lies buried
His a voice of reason through Imperial expansion
Dealt harshly by the Crown during the North West Rebellion
When convicted of treason by a court in his land

Canadian ideals were the order of the day
Ancient values and worth were just in the way
Poundmaker's reasoned thought didn't hold any sway
And the forces of the Crown made First Nations prey

Today the great chief is honoured by all
As a Statesman and Peacemaker in Canada's halls
Exonerated, Poundmaker still lifts high the peace sign
And shaken was History as she rewrites events of the time

(reading Treaty 6 will give an insight into Poundmaker's world)

Women at Risk

Written following the US Supreme Court decision to reverse Roe V. Wade, but the poem can equally apply to all women everywhere.

The creators, the courageous, and those at first base
Women at risk over millennia through man's bloody quakes
From childhood to bearing the future race
Childbirth throughout history was never an easy break

But yet courage, resolve, and sacrifice
Carries women through the greatness of life
Bearing the brunt of others who throw the dice
Putting women in the cross-hairs of much needless strife

Should there not be an end to women taking it on the chin
When risk is one way and they have no say
And laws made by men making women at risk spin
Though their spirit is a birthright but not theirs to play

Chapter 4
Ice

The Columbia Ice Field

On top of the Columbia Ice Field in the mid 1950's showing the Bombardier B12 snowmobile which took us up the glacier, (from the author's collection).

Ice flows have parted from their polar birth
Faster now in the fever of steaming Earth
And glaciers crash down the valleys of time
And waters from millennia flow down the divide
Warming seas and oceans and creating new lines
Between water and land and risking life-kind

March of the Icebergs

The Arctic's icebergs of never-ending might
Run to the south in columns at night
Only a fraction seen over the waves
Their mountainous steeples high above in white

In magnificent lines down Earth's meridians
Like men o' war floating in deadly procession
Dangerous to many if unseen in the sea
And raging against the world once they break free

The harbinger of change from the Arctic waters
Coming from their northern home which is no longer free
For the enemy has plundered the Arctic and its tundras
And Icebergs break off on their way south in the sea

If ever there was a worry in the world, we now see
The march of the icebergs gives us a vision of "to be"
Breaking off in their thousands from the Arctic seas
The ice of the ancients is bleeding by man's heavy knee

March of the Icebergs (In Haiku)

Arctic ice melts fast
Icebergs are breaking away
The north is weeping

The Icicle

A glistening steeple pointed to earth
The sun makes it glow as nature gives birth
Growing with time as weather blossoms forth
The icicle a symbol of those in the north.

Waxing and waning with the sun's cold sheen
Falling drops of water in bright light glitter
A translucent spike through which sunlight is seen
Clear brilliant ice where prisms shimmer

There but a moment in time transfixed
A symbol of winter in glowing relief
A bright-lit lance piercing winter betwixt
Sky and earth like a diamond leaf

Gone for the season but waiting the earth's might
Reborn next year when a cool sun will glow
Through a pointed arrow that brings such light
For eyes that can see through winters snow

Chapter 5
War

de Havilland Mosquito FB26-KA114, built in Canada in 1945 and restored to flying condition (photograph courtesy of Jim Rayner.

Mosquito Sortie

Or The Wooden Wonder

7781 de Havilland Mosquitos were built, including 1032 in Canada. It was the fastest piston-engine aircraft for much of World War ll. Only a handful are left, including one at the Aviation Museum in Ottawa.

Their history is immense; what a sight to see one fly.

Arrow straight out over the Channel
At sea level, setting a course towards Hell
Carrying war to destroy black enemy trammel
For when Mosquitos flew, they rang the enemy death knell

What fearsome power those wooden wings bore
Flying from England over the occupied French shore
Targets selected to destroy the enemy as did Thor
The Wooden Wonder flew for peace and to end all war

Far-reaching in design to carry total war to the fight
Ranging far over Europe in the deadly black night
There was nowhere the Merlins couldn't take their might
Towards distant targets, then home, and England in sight

Living now in history but made alive by memories
Of aircrew who lived to write about their wings of the night
Just a few survive brought to life for future centuries
The Mosquito aircraft, one of peace's deadly white knights

The Ultimate Weapon

What causes some to demand all to follow
Their beliefs which to others may seem hollow
Using power to order and to satisfy an itch
That only they can see is the right way to pitch

Opinions striking out more warlike than ever
With greater risk of outcomes that might well sever
Mankind from a quiet life bowing to pressure
As non-reason rules the world in ever greater measure

So many events where a threat has risen
More dangerous than any could possibly reckon
For actions against the people, the people must stiffen
Making The Rule Of Law, the ultimate weapon

Guns of March

(Written at the start of the Russian invasion of Ukraine)

Up in the building looking over the park
In the distance, the river flows blue in the light
Warm once more, the birds are making their mark
Flashing splinters of colour as arrows in flight

The sound of the birds in orchestral might
Perched in the trees or on wires and poles
Cacophonous sounds in the green spring light
Tiny harbingers from the sky in giant's roles

Migratory geese gliding by in perfect formation
Seagulls soaring high riding thermals in delight
Cardinals and chickadees and sparrows of our nation
Flying free in our lands as is their birthright

Hardy in winter if they stay with the snow
So strong in migration as they fly south on the globe
Returning north to the tundras to live and grow
Through trees and mountains and waterways they probe.

Where would we be without our feathered winged wonders
Free of the earth by the design of uncounted eons
Roaming the world in their colourful numbers
Watching fools invade Ukraine with their marauding legions

The Guns of March darken Ukraine's new spring
But little birds with their wings rise above the gun's thunder
Still building their nests to raise new sky kings
Flying cycles of life where we watch them in wonder

War Tulips Of The Netherlands or Along The Rideau Way

Every year in Ottawa
Along the Rideau way

Bulbs are set from far horizons
Holland's tulips in their thousands

Waiting till the winter has passed
And the canal is free to flow at last

The bulbs begin to show the green
Of life emerging in a vibrant sheen

Brilliant colour in many arrays
Viewed in their many thousand displays

Red, orange, purple and yellow
As pleasing in tone as a humming cello

They are a poem of remembrance
Of Canada's great war presence

In Holland

Destruction

Destruction has moved to the Middle East
Around The Mediterranean's old and bloody shores
Bombs and bullets are giving a new blood feast
Fed by policy, opinion, money, terrorism, and war

None to climb the mountain of peace
When mired in the mud of human destruction
None reaching to the future to give release
And only a few are triggering war's mindless suction

None in the world body of the nations of man
None seeing any light in the endless strife of mankind
None to say "no", its time to draw a line in the sand
Are there any to see the way forward when all are so blind

And Still the Hammer Falls
Or The Children Of Gaza

Children cry but the hammer still falls
No matter the arm that wields the blows
The strike is blind from righteous halls
As anguish rages for the blood of children in red flows

The explosions are too big to escape the terror bombs
The bullets are too fast shot in hails of crossfire
Causing souls of our children to rise in heaven too fast
As justice on Earth burns on war's smoking pyre

The War Train, or The Woman At The Station

The poem was written following the invasion of Ukraine.

A black locomotive is steaming in the dark before light
In front of never-ending cars way down the long track
Massive steel, iron wheels, and driving pistons waiting fire
As a woman stands waiting for the war train to go back

Not alone waiting for a loved one to leave
Others in quiet silence, wait for the train to take
Soldiers to fight in a conflict beyond what we believe
Events that overwhelm, now life or death is at stake

Women left at home watching distance unfold
Silently wondering as they stand in quiet worry
Eyes turned toward the train waiting to roll
Alone and lonely in the station's loud hurry

Clear eyes and face upwards to the blue sky now shining
The train bound for the front with destiny's army aboard
She is alone with a melody of quiet crescendos perhaps defining
A Rachmaninoff love song played in whispering chords

Now, in the distance for the war train has moved
Taking soldiers to arm and defend a bleeding nation
A strong woman left alone, resolute but war-bruised
Waiting to return again to the train at the station

War in Ukraine

Cracking, cracking, the bullets are flying
Sounds sounds the children are crying
Bombing bombing the buildings are crashing
Standing standing defiant eyes are flashing

Fighting fighting against invading war hordes
Holding holding brittle armies at the gates
Defending defending your cities from thousands
Striding striding with resolve to war madness

Never never halter rights to just lives
Oppose oppose tireless in your strengths
The world the world is behind your resolves
Always always we will give you helplines

Invaders, Invaders, what are your whys
Killing killing other people's free lives
Where where are you when your army expires
Alone alone on the worlds vast stage

Stop stop the madness of your tremors
Power power will not fly from your borders
Where where will you fit in peoples hearts
When when the war machine halts

Better better we must manage the days
Never never give up on worlds peoples
Create create new vibrant world orders
Life life for all is more than wills of dictators

Chapter 6
The Maritimes

"The North Atlantic viewed from Port Morien, Cape Breton, Nova Scotia" (from the author's collection).

Sea Life of Old Nova Scotia

Inspired by two of W.R. MacAskill's photographs of Nova Scotia
-The Starboard Lookout and
-Kingdom By The Sea

The starboard lookout in the schooner's bow
Tied to a mast as the vessel plows
Through storms and spray that hits the prow
He guarded the ship's life with salt furrowed brow

The days of sail on the Nova Scotia coasts
Saw little ships crafted with skills that could boast
Voyages in northern waters or down south to roast
The fishermen of Nova Scotia sailed with old ocean ghosts

Gone are the days of little kingdoms by the sea
For a vibrancy was there in life on the quay
In cottages and shops and boatworks on the lea
In houses and gardens and hard life that was free

Black Rum

The ancient trade of the eastern route
Salt fish from cold Nova Scotia homes
Ships to Jamaica and the Caribbean set sail
For sugar and molasses the ships did roam

Black rum and sugar were the trade front line
North along coasts of green new lands
Rum, lumber, furs, and fish in the brine
A part of life along Atlantic shore sands

With fistfuls of butter and handfuls of brown sugar
And a few pints of black rum in a wooden bucket
Mixed in heaven with spices and boiled water or cider
Warming North Woods people like big gold nuggets

Hot rum held one warm on heavy bleak nights
Two mugs enough to stop lone thoughts of hard life
Steaming beakers to warm edges of the mind
Boiling Black Rum allowing the spirit to unwind*

*The toddy recipe although not original to North America having
originated in India, is loosely based on the recipe in Kenneth Robert's
book Northwest Passage

Canadian Rum Runners

What a boon to intrepid Canadians
The US ban on freedom's liquor generated
Fast boats to take spirits to thirsty Americans
Much ingenuity and daring was ultimately created

The little fast boats with big aircraft engines
Plied the saltwater coasts of the Atlantic and Pacific
In the rumrunning glide over the intricate tides
Rum was welcome to Americans but to police horrific

What madness occurred in the banning of booze
That was drank for millennia beside fires in the cold
A botanical marvel turning water into wine
Or the magic of sugar in making rum to run the tide

The running of rum provided many needy families with loot,
Aside from the adventure the speed of the boats gave
To those sneering at a ban giving booze the boot
They ran a sea-born rum river the US did crave

The View From the Window Sydney NS

From the author's collection

Yesterday the snow was falling
In swaths of white at night
Lighting on trees and houses
Shining bright in evening light

Calm and steady the snowflakes fell
No wind to disturb the sight
A carpet of snow delighting the senses
As the night descended in quiet might

The day arrived and the snowfall shone
On all the trees as the light peered through
Warming the eyes as the shadows rose
Giving shades of white in morning's bright blue

Tomorrow We Leave Cape Breton

Or Beyond Canadian Horizons

St. Ann's Harbour, Cape Breton (from the author's collection).

Tomorrow we leave Cape Breton
Taking a final look at the sea
Watching the brilliance of clouds
Reaching far horizons so free

The fishing boats on this January day
Lying calm in the harbour at Main a Dieu
Under the sky so blue and white
Taking the mind through history as it flew

Thinking of peace and the calm
On the Canadian Eastern coast
The clouds have been there for lifetimes
Messengers from heaven's post

Shades of grey and white so bright
Gracing the shore in heavenly might
The surf beating free that none can slight
Atlantic Canada there in peaceful sight

Bent to the wind in a mighty blast
The surf is crashing in thunderous sound
Like war and violence beyond our shores
But on Canada's horizons peace is crown

Chapter 7
Poems Inspired By Art And Music

Emily Carr

A British Columbian woman, an artist on the West Coast
Created great forests of Canada in paintings of green
Life on the docks, and totems of First Nation's hosts
Preserving forever titan images of Canadian scenes

It took a lifetime for her work to be deemed of mind's worth
A period of time in which she described herself as "small"
Her little grave is remembered in Victoria as "she of the earth"
As plain as Van Gogh's in Anvers-Sur-Oise by a wall

What is it about visionaries rendering life's pictures creating
A lifetime of work in making art for minds and eyes
For others viewing what the artist's senses were stating
Creating for them "what was" when the future does arise

One of the first environmentalists as seen through her images
Of British Columbia forests and oceans in green and blue hues
And structures and totems by the sea of the First Villages
Her vibrant view of nature slumbered until her art broke through

Let all those great artists creating images so personal
Whose driven ideals never stop over long working years
Be remembered in the history of art as artists subliminal
And be revered as those who have given us emotion and tears

Emily Carr (in Haiku)

Blackgreen stars of earth
Forests forged in paintings
Brushstrokes for our minds

Morning

This poem was inspired by Pier Gynt Suite 1, Opus 46, 1, Morning Mood, composed by Edvard Greig.

Rising melodies sounding thin in early light
Flow over the fjords majestic in sight
Rippling the water as the sound takes wing
Giving emotion to all as waking minds start to sing

Gaining strength as the sun rises over the mountains
Causing shadows to flee as shorelines become clear
The music fills the senses like glittering fountains
For the beauty of Norway can bring many a tear

Rising in crescendos as the sun breaks free
Seen over the hills in the new light of day
The music hovering as clouds top the horizon
Filling the fjord where longships were once aweigh

The horns blast the fjord on the way to the coast
Showing sea paths to the ocean drawn by orchestral strings
With melodies kissing mountains where sheep and goats are host
Norway in the morning, where dragons once had wings

The Condor

This poem was inspired by the timeless music of El Condor
Pasa composed by Daniel A. Robles in 1914.

Over the endless granite rock of the Andes
Climbing sunwards to towering heights
Through high valleys and passes of copper
The condor rides thermals in flight

Their wings grant the spirit of freedom
Never bothered by walls of rock
Soaring high over the valleys in air
Flying endlessly in winds unlocked

The winds never say where they blow
But the condor soars with them to know
Upwards in currents to the clouds
Downwards to the mountains below

The haunting melody of the condors
Known over the world as free
Not bothered by puny man
Their wings have never bent a knee

From The Crags and the Glens and the Sea

This poem was inspired by Dougie McLean's composition "The Gael."

Rising from the sea to the Scottish Highlands
Swirling through lochs and streams and over the falls
A melody from history reaches the kilted bands
When the pipes and drums from old crags call

The pipes are singing echoing the winds of the past
From where else could such music raise Scotland's mast
Like words of the great Robbie lashing wealth and class
In poems lasting forever, telling the Scot's story at last

The lament is blown by winds carrying the songs
Over the world where the Scots came from beyond
For the melodies of Scotland gave new music and belonged
With the breath of the pipes and the drum beats that awed

Gardens

This poem was inspired by Monte Don's television programs on Gardens.

Long before the seven wonders were built by mankind
Far back in history garden art forms did shine
Of symmetries in green giving peace to ancient minds
Calming man's thoughts making gardens into shrines

Beautiful gardens once built for priests and kings
Of hedges and paths and ponds and meditation rings
Beyond the view of the many who weren't seen to think of great things
The carved structures of gardens gave the privileged some wings

Zen gardens of the far east with their simplicity and empty space
Abstracts in rock, cultured gravel, flowers and moss
Tended with devotion to contemplate the meaning of life
In temples of serenity and peace without strife

Man's gardens for crops growing vegetables and fruits
Giving food for the year in delicate rows harbouring roots
Or fields of water around mountains rising high growing rice
Muscles and sweat giving man life from a hoed paradise

But what of the mountains and forests, plains and oceans
Painted by nature given symmetry by seasons and eons
With the sun, moon, sky, and thunderous empty space
Where is seen the magnificent garden of our ancient earth

Steam

The poem was inspired by J. M. W. Turner's painting
Rain, Steam, Speed, The Great Western Railway, housed in
the National Gallery. London UK.

Fire deep in a belly enclosed in iron
Stoked continually with wood, coal, and chaff
A new purpose to create a pyre
To heat some water, make it boil and laugh

That iron belly needed some strength
It wasn't for nothing the cauldron was braced
Too much fire would cause it's breath
To explode outwards as wild steam raced

Massive steel bolts held the iron together
Thick steel plates were welded as one
A boiler holding water and fire in a strong tether
Until steam formed and set the engine to run

Gauges were needed to determine the force
And valves designed that blew over pressure
The steam was controlled, a man made horse
Ready to pull with god-like action measured

Installed in a mine, on a rail, or ship at sea
A force for work as a pump, a wheel or a paddle
Water was boiled, making steam scream like a banshee
The magic of pressure harnessed, and dazzled

Bigger and bigger, and faster and faster
The world narrowed down but steam expanded
Factories are powered, steam a taskmaster
People to cities, the country empty-handed

Steam met a challenge as peoples rose
Keeping pace with industry, science and structure
Heating, lighting, powering, cities in new roles
There was nowhere it wasn't always much stronger.

While invention moves on and there is new prime movers
Steam will remain as a force forever
New applications, along with the old
As long as there's heat it will remain in favour

J.M.W. Turner (In Haiku)

Fire, steam, speed, in paint
Above arts' understanding
There for future years

Blossoms

This poem was inspired by Chopin's Nocturn in C Sharp Minor.

In colours across the spectrum of light
Petals burst in harmony in man's limited sight
Fleeting glimpses of the continuance of might
As nature from eons flows in earth's spring flight

Like the vibrant tones from a harp or piano
Played to take the mind onwards to nirvana
Blossoms will fall striking earth like a bell
In silent tones as man watches nature's life knell

Walking in peace on carpets of white, red, or green
Maybe cherry blossoms or dogwood or redbuds seen
Each with a tone that resonates in the mind
For the music of nature helps all to unwind

The Giants of Rapa Nui

Or The Easter Island Moai

Countless thoughts of modern man over many long years
Have wondered at the heads of their volcanic peers
Words and shovels seek the secrets of centuries
Carved long ago by artists, these ancient antiquities

Has research over time and deduction
Discerned the truth of the giants construction
Watching oceans and seas for masts or enemies
Providing food and protection over many centuries

What was the reason of the hard rock carvings
In style and content of what was evolving
Were the heads original, affected not by ancients
Or built on images from all the compass radians

For thousands of years did art build on art
Forms with changing ideas of mind and heart
Art in the West in the Dark Ages was stilted
When the giants were born far in the Pacific

Did the stone works of India, Angkor or Polynesia
Provide an art bridge to the new in Rapa Nui
Or was imagery borrowed from Aztec, Incan, or Mayan
For ancient art creations no matter where were never forsaken

Drawings by mankind since the time of caves
Testament of minds to make records of the days
Memory images of the deepest in the mind's spirit
Lasting forever making the artist's works explicit

The great mystery of art which has never ceased
And continues on as mankind's thoughts are released
And Rapa Nui heads watched a stretch of the Pacific
Over winds and waves hiding the ocean's hieroglyphics

Vision unlimited by mountain or forest
Watching, watching, the horizon's far chorus

Tom Thomson

Tom is gone now but the pines still whisper
Canada's lakes in vibrant blues continue to glimmer
Through birches and leaves in the fall that shimmer
Waiting for new brushstrokes before becoming dimmer

To paint the leaves falling on the Canadian Shield
Seen around the world in red, silver and green
Never to be forgotten his forests continue to gleam
Where is the artist to record again a wilderness so clean

What was in his mind that was there undrawn
In images of Canada that beckoned his brush
Still, nature's coloured palette is there in the dawn
As seasons wait to be painted in their earthly blush

The Sea woman

There are four statues of Gudrid and Snorri in various places in Europe and North America from which this poem was inspired. The one I saw was at Library and Archives Canada in Ottawa.

The Viking sagas and empirical evidence indicate she crossed the Atlantic several times in the 10th century and while once living in France she walked from there to Rome and back. She was the first European woman to give birth in Canada at the Viking settlement of L'Anse aux Meadows in Northern Newfoundland along the Straits of Belle Isle

What did she in the longship see
Watching from the dragon with emotion
As the coast to be Canada came free
For a place to land safe from the ocean

What a beauty, crusted with spray
Bearing hard to shore with sail close hauled
Oars were set and she began to give way
Towards the beach, where a new land called

Here a thousand years ago she gave birth
The first of Europe in Canada
Gudrid, the far-travelled, from Iceland's earth
Her home in the North Atlantic

The longship home-bound was given its course
Back to Iceland, a ship of the Red Saga
But Gudrid made the mark with Snorri and the Norse
A sea woman; part of the vision of Canada

The Sea woman (In Haiku)

Gudrid and Snorri

The sea woman lands
On Canada's Belle Isle Strait
A thousand years past

Chapter 8
Some Reflections on History, Nature and The Signs of Our Times

Born on the Shortest Day of the Year

Poem written for our daughter using an expression written by an old friend and neighbour when she was born.

Born on the shortest day of the year
When sunlight dims for the last time
For next day a new year bursts forth
And a new life begins to chime

Born on the shortest day of the year
Gives peace through the longest night
Moving into the new day without fear
As the world opens up with newborn sight

Retirement

Retirement flies
Earth and sky in our eyes

No clouds unmoving
We are improving
The lot

Tomorrow is brilliant

Wings

Waking to a bird song following the night
Their colours seen through trees or along the bight
Perched on a low branch or in a tree at height
Their songs of the morning gets one out in the light

The flights go on through skies dark or blue
Hardy the birds are as they fly day and night
Resting in nests that are hidden from view
Or soaring in bright colours to our endless delight

Broad wings of great eagles light in the wind
Or the beat of the songbird nimble in sight
Or the arrow of the peregrine in a downward fight
Or the honk of wild geese in continental flight

The glide of the seabirds hovering over the waves
The flight of the Albatross, the Tern, the Swift
Seeing the world over as they roam, ever brave
Flying over the oceans as their wings soar in airlifts

The colour of birds is an eye's delight going forth
Singing away for us all searching for grass or seeds
Moving with speed either to the south or the north
Following the colour of seasons going wherever they please

A new season has started and the winds come alive
As winged creatures fill the mind in gracing the sky
Magical beings a delight in their never-ending drive
As songs fill the air when the birds are on high

Books

Even very young
A book is a wonder
The pages sprung
Turning like thunder
Adventures from a character
Riding forever
Under the covers with a light.

The Pessimist

Bleak minds of some
Can't see a glimmer

Of light over there and around
As its hard to see and is out of bounds

Not caused by destiny
Just spinning grey

Come into the light,
All sides are so bright

There is room to stray
In the light of day

The Player Plays

The street musician
Hovers over his shadow
Thinking of times past
About to play a staccato

The chords strike out
Causing passers-by to stop
Listening in silence
As the player plays non-stop

Never a missed or incorrect beat
The fingers fly through the remembered chords
Strings or keys all in tune and complete
Out on the street, so masterfully scored

Where was the talent earned, maybe with tears
Maybe in an orchestra he chose not to surmount
What was missing there over many past years
To come to the street to let what was in him out

The thrill of music was given to passer-by people
Waiting for sounds with anticipated pleasure
As the player played on through his symphonic easel
Returning tomorrow to create a new musical treasure

Big Events

We are not seeing cataclysmic events
Here in the West, under democratic tents
That affect our well-being just going to a store
To buy what we want from products galore

There aren't any land mines as we walk out the door
Planted by armies to blow up our kids on the shore
No cracking of bullets against old church stone walls
No one is stopping us from walking free in our halls

Yet there are elements about as one watches the airwaves
Of anger and non-truths in our world not of slaves
Violent will is expanding and doing much harm
The simple past is as gone as a quiet life on the farm

When we walk the streets, no warplanes are flying
Buildings are standing with no bombs loudly blasting
No dead in our streets that are left crumbled in dust
Caused by aggression and war where there wasn't any trust

What will happen if the bombs start dropping
Here in the West where freedom is basking
And big events start war trains of armies in tasking
Defence of the nation and render irrelevant
Trifles that confound us now no longer resonant

Separation of Church and State

The pope made a statement about religious might
To those amongst us who wanted to exercise a right
Calling abortion the result of hiring a hitman to kill
Where according to the Church no lives should be spilled

As in all things about power the memory can be short
As events unfold causing some to extort
Compliance by those who differ from religious rules
Negating the law separating state from church views

Modern law was constructed to separate the church and the state
It should not be clouded by those who believe opening that gate
For to do so will back all of us a thousand years
And nothing will be left except an ocean of tears

Cell Phones Personified

Held to the ear the eye is blind
Or as fingers flash in texting mode
The eyes are tunneled and both ears deaf
When Cells head out with their talkers in tow

Sooner or later crossing a street in town
Cells on the move might bring a driver down
By a heart attack that will cause the driver to pound
The talker while the driver is dead to sound

What about locomotive horns that can ennoble sound
When Cells start transmitting and brains are drowned
And peripheral vision is lost with eyes focused down
Giving a blast to the talkers that will crack their crowns

Imagine Cells fumbled in trembling fingers shaken
And febrile knees might weaken tossing Cells in the air
And talkers worry that their Cell Masters have been taken
By ghost trains from nowhere as their godly horns do blare

Voice Mail Stops Business Cold

Heaven sent voices of money efficiency tell you to wait
While electronic devils determine your fate
When you bleed over menus and voices that prate
That give you options that may not always be great

Anything to save a buck in the world where we live
No person available to talk to you to sift
Information you need to pass through the sieve
To the end of the line to those who can give

Finally there, at the end to "the voice" that matters
And Voice Mail tells you to message the phone's ear
But by now, the mind and body is reduced to tatters
Bruising a brain that can only be helped with a beer

The Angel's Share

Or Scotch Whisky

A new cask was laid down in a rocky little town
Full of the malt that brews in a little building so brown
A cask filled to the brim and not a drop ever wasted
The bung in the hole was set waiting for that which god created

Only the distiller knew of the quality of the brew
That waited among cobwebs in casks set in pews
Row upon row getting brown with old whisky
The barrels waited aging, their malts getting frisky

But not only the master who set the malt down
Knew of the quality of the brew he just crowned
For up in the blue perched on clouds with no sound
Scottish angels looked down their wings quivering for a round

With wings folded tight and gowns streaming white
Like arrows they dropped to the little building with delight
Drifting through doors and hallways to barrels awaiting their plight
Those angels weren't above having a few drams that night

Over the years as Scotch Whiskey in ancient woods aged
The angels took turns quaffing beakers from the barrels caged
Sniffing the bouquets of the heather and the peats as time waged
The Angels took a share and diminished Time's magic unweighed

Their Angel's Share was chugged with horns raised in good cheer
And with wings beating feebly and drunk without fear
They managed the climb back to those clouds without a tear
Knowing tomorrow there will be a new cask without peer

The John Deere 730

A boy was fortunate when living in a town
To go with his Dad to a country farm
For there in a field that needed the plow
A big tractor waited with a strong green arm

Man's inventions of engines gave power to the tire
Long gone the draft of man, ox and horse
For horsepower was harnessed by energy on fire
As yellow wheels were geared to the heavy torque force

What a treat for a kid to sit
On a big green tractor when four plows behind bit
Turning over green sod for the diesel never quit
Looking over his shoulder at sod the plow split

The heavy crack of two pistons more powerful than Thor
Was the sound of its engine giving musical thumps
Eleven hundred and twenty-five revs at full bore
Under full load its beat never ceasing as it jumps

Such are the memories of a youth in the light
Not many had the privilege that kid had with his dad
Those long-gone years helped make the future bright
And long hours on the 730 were shortened by delight

Memories of Youth

Memories of a distant past
Of distant shores that will always last
Or around the corner and down the street
The road was long and life was sweet

Memories of mountains and hills and trees
Of oceans and beaches warm in the breeze
Or rivers and fish that jump to the skies
Of life across vistas that never dies

Ah youth, where memories live and fly
Never forgotten no matter the sigh
Moving upwards and onwards the future's bright
For the past is here and memories can take flight

We cannot forget how life turns and twists
But we are here our span to persist
And those coming after will be a bright light
And theirs the turn to live the fight

For Jaguar Lovers

Never-ending back pain is a little bit iffy
The knees are a bit stiff and the cane is in hand
Swinging the legs aboard is a little bit tricky
But your Jaguar waits ready to ride the land

Eyes are focused and no matter how old
They glitter with fervour as the engine roars
Gripping the wheel with arthritic hands so cold
With a foot on the throttle all ready for war

British Racing Green and a supercharger in hand
The Jaguar begins to move as the throttle expands
Years forgotten as the wheels roll down the road
Nothing like a Jag to warm those arthritic cold hands

Keep them going guys, there will never be the like
Of old British wheels on the great turnpikes
The magic of a marque blasting down the road
Causes heads to turn as the big Cat strikes

www.ingramcontent.com/pod-product-compliance
Lightning Source LLC
Chambersburg PA
CBHW042305070726

47818CB00009B/230